SALUTE

Friends Pam Brown, Laurie Duggan and Tim Wright have given advice—that clearly I have not always taken—as well as encouragement (that many will feel to have been contra-indicated). My thanks to these poets.

ACKNOWLEDGEMENTS

'Late At Night—Bruny Island' first appeared in *Cordite*
'2.12.08—Poem for Philip Whalen' appeared in *JACKET2* and later the *Journal of Poetics Research*.
'New Way Of Worrying', and 'What's Best' appeared first in *JACKET2;*
'Salute' in *Australian Book Review*
'*Re* Peter Black' & 'Starting near the cakeshop' appeared in *Sport* (NZ)
'Hi, Small Bug' in *Australian Poetry journal*

My thanks to the editors of these magazines

SALUTE

KEN BOLTON

PUNCHER & WATTMANN

First published in 2019
Published by Puncher and Wattmann
PO Box 279
Waratah NSW 2298

http://www.puncherandwattmann.com
puncherandwattmann@bigpond.com

ISBN: 9781925780406

 A catalogue record for this book is available from the National Library Australia.

Cover design by Miranda Douglas
Cover image—*Strada di Parigi*,1934 by Filippo de Pisis
Text design by Christine Bruderlin
Printed by Lightning Source International

  This project has been assisted by the Australian Government through the Australia Council, its arts funding and advisory body.

Contents

I *

DUTY CHART

I remember just before I
go to sleep: I left my bus ticket
in my back pocket—the ticket
I hardly ever use.
I wonder
briefly—
& remember why I have remembered this:
I was trying to think
what I'd done today—
shopped, which I'd done
with Cath (who reads, now,
beside me). And who moves
& turns off her light.
I dug a circle round
the lemon tree prior to
moving it in a week or two, or three,
cleaned up after yesterday's
pruning job on the almond,
cut some wood. An
electrician came—
to approve work some others
had done: 'sign off' on it.
We talked to him. Petted Pola,
had lunch. I ironed
a bit & cooked dinner
a Greek rice-&-eggplant thing
I've been making for thirty years,
read Frederic Raphael's anger on behalf
of Irene Nemirovsky (in fact
I've been reading Sebald's books

four of them in quick succession. The
Holocaust "never goes away", as Cath remarks—
you can think, No more! But there is always
another facet, another account
that will claim your attention.) The
day. On my mind—Pam, &
a lot of other friends: I've had to
write about them all just recently.
(I seem to have been 'despatching jobs'
remarkably effectively.) Now I think about them—
a sudden family from the past:
how are they all? Like
children who have moved away,
around the globe, far from home.
I was not their father—*in any way*—
but I remember them all as young
(as they were when I knew them).
(As I was.) Are they
well, prospering? sad? happy?
Pam, tho, I do know. She never drifted.
Pam, are you okay?

Part Two
Another one of those poems where I
end on a question

                    so, effectively, the
whole poem
                   is a kind of feeling towards
its end,

what it 'has-to-say'.

                                    Fine
if that is interesting enough, in its
'own right'
                (almost never)
                                    or if the search
was enough of a journey
                        — & tensions, connections, are
resolved by it.

                                    Best if
I'm surprised myself.
                        Indicating
'Home at last'?
                    'Dig here'?
(or 'Go to bed!'
                    the Edith Sitwell quote.
why did I attribute it
                    to her?
fun:
        the upper crust name.
                                'Home at last'
                                    means
formal resolution
                        Tho not,
Necessarily, much more
                        ('Dig here'—
the implication is 'depths'.

                        ('Dig
here' means, effectively, nearly always,

5

                                   for me,
                    "down tools!"
                                        & like unionised
                                           labour
     my mind walks off the job.
                                   We'll fish another day)
     Jenny Bornholdt often seems to have
          'a good talk' with a taxi driver—
          the Wellington taxi drivers being very wise.
     The one (page 70) who likes "the sound of the world"
                         (because it has 'reason' in it)
                         (i.e., rather than radio, music etc)
                              There was a time
                                   when
     Taxi! Crab & I would shout. In the pub—whenever
     the conversation got too boring.
     (The Little Richard song—
                    "Taxi, taxi—take me
     anywhere"
                    on my mind back then.

          Ah, Crab.

TWO MELBOURNE POEMS, JUNE 2012

In Another Town
I am puzzled,
by emotions
I can't do
anything with.
(Not My Town.)
      Down-
stairs the sound
of the footy Shan
& John watch.
1) Melbourne's
sentiment for art.
2) The reading, that
went so well. And I go
(I will go)
back—
to home
& Adelaide— 3),
with the memory of it.
And 4) Brunswick Street,
Helen & Peter. Ros
& *Kinky Jurlinki*
John & Ann, &
their students—the
poets who will be next,
smart, kind,
sympathetic, to whom
I read, better read
than me—with it
'all before them'

& so whom I love they
look so heroic tho
not, of course, to
themselves Tim,
Duncan, Tina,
Caroline, Sam & Corey
        all of a piece
with the photos of
an earlier avant-garde
                that
I never cared much
for. But whom I
like—in their
photographs—lean
simply dressed
handsome & plain,
in their shirts &
dresses &
dedication
to possibility &
each other, the
promise they mostly
missed, fell short of

there is something
'glowing' about it
I never assented
to before. Danilla,
Nolan, Hester,
Matchan Skipper.

I see the Whissons
—& like them less,
but I like them;
Vassilieff brings
a tincture of
Europe—that fades,
abandons him: a
life sentimental
for us but
soured for him I
imagine.
          Coffee
& chips, with John,
& we go to the reading
& give it. Life for
us.

Second Poem
Often the
second poem
is the one that
lifts takes off.
That would be good,
as Pam said—
cause that would be
this, this one.
Me, seated,
under a harsh light
in bed—a little

'like' the picture of
Forbes I gave,
Forbes conflated with
the Guston portrait
('self-portrait')—the
late night worrier.
Who?—you say—*Me?*
John?? Philip Guston? All
of us? Yes.
Settling for
very little, happily—
having thought about
Vassilieff—the promise,
mild I guess, that
didn't come off. He brought
some Parisian lightness as
of Bonnard, something
guileless as well that asked
to be accepted, that proved
not enough. Act as if
the world exists, the Surrealists
said. It, certainly, won't act
as if you did &
me, I am barely here.
Tho happy at this moment.

II *

2/12/08 — A POEM FOR PHILIP WHALEN

"Here it comes again, imagination of myself"
Philip Whalen, 'International Date Line, Monday / Monday 27:IX:67'

Here it comes again, imagination of myself:
I sit, in the harsh light, in a study
(mine)

It's the light I like,
& it's late.

"In a study" always suggests "He was in
a bad mood, tense with it"—not that—
reading Whalen, a book of drawings by Kirchner,

the Berlin Street Scenes—in an attempt
to gain *some* purchase, kick off
from something different—thinking

of Yuri, a bit, Cath's eldest son, the one
I know least but like & like his difficult life
& how he's dealt with it. *"Yuri—I will speak*

with you later!" My friends the poets, famous,
in their way—in the not very satisfying way available
to them (some)—large in my mind at any rate—

& another, rather foolish, at the same time as
rather good—well, alternately, from poem to poem—
something of a comeback. Another friend, ill

seriously mortally time running out. How quickly? How
quickly for all of us, the question. ('A' question.) Anna, &
boyfriend Chris, on their anger at / fascination with

13

The Howard Years documentary a
self-serving account but, as they say, so far
the major & lone political fact of their lives

It will be their early history: *yech*—Reith,
Howard himself (whom I never expected
in the 80s I would have to hate—what future

did *he* have?). The rest.
'Consigned' now 'to oblivion'—to echo & re-echo
in succeeding waves

of revision, counter-construal,

like analyses of the Third Republic, the French
Second Empire. Where are we now? Even 'interesting times'
seem to follow a pattern—the bangs & whimpers

louder, more ironically conventional for their
inadequacy to the occasion. Will America go under
because of Bush? how appropriate

But was that my point? Late at night,
not even worrying. Whalen . . . the Kirchner drawings.

Go under? What,
next week?

Okay, then.

"It may never happen!" Isn't that the joke?
If it takes ten years, if it takes twenty,
it will be cataclysmic. Tho—(20 years)—

I might be out of the way—or less concerned by then.
If curious as to the outcomes. For
twenty years —for thirty— amused

—"amused at best"—

by Whalen's politics—when I thought of them—
the raves & rants, observations,
of a hippy dropout. Well, a Beat

the one I like best. What did Whalen change?

He was sane, he set an example. Now,
as I read the poems, I find those same politics
both nostalgic & to the point.

What will I change—
if I put my crazy-arse shoulder to the wheel?
Is the answer: "In *this* vassal state?"

Or
"You should have thought of this earlier"?

Leave a record, like Whalen did,
of clear perceptions. The avowedly
political—Naomi Klein, Tony Negri—seem no

nearer the mark, tho fun to think about, think
with. Negri, so systematic, abstract, & wishful.
(The 'Multitude'—what a category! How do I join, ha ha.)

The overweening confidence & blindness of
think-tank America: the End of History.
Self-deluded—& the rest of the world knew.

(Cheney, Rumsfeld, the others—*Pal,*
we make history!)

A century
of Interesting Times. More. Beginning when?
1871? 1789?

The innocence, & the percipience,
of my artistic heroes seems so touching,
even their blindness. Manet O'Hara Coltrane

—loons like de Chirico—the Germans, Kirchner
Kokoschka, Adorno—Christa Wolf. Did they each sit up,
as I do, in bed—a sleeping other at their side—

writing, nodding off . . . ?

The fan is going & blows my page occasionally,
though I have weighted it now with *Heavy Breathing,*
Whalen's orange-covered volume,

with its wonderful drawing . . . that is too smart
to date much, really. Then one day it will date
suddenly—the ironies, the humour, the seriousness

will cease to register—a fallen, a trashed
civilization. I hope not. Tho Whalen of course
could live with it. Less tied to this world than me.

I *like* life. I like 'the continuing story', anyway,
& will be unhappy about it, the rupture. Will
the rest of my life prepare me? ("Check the serenity!"

Ha ha ha. Dreaming?)
My body, turning, in some future.

Now I read this 24 hours later, & rub Cath's
beautiful shoulder. If I "love life"

why haven't I had one—like Whalen did?
Tho I must've—mine's all <u>gone</u>, right?
In fact I don't know much about what Whalen did.

I seem to have spent mine day-dreaming—or thinking 'hard'
about music, blues & jazz, & art—& making jokes & quipping
& making poems out of it. The women

I've hung around have kept me sane. (A few were
'nuts' — but I was nuttier.)

People just want to be happy? The big,
noble notions
exist, it sometimes seems, as 'a caution', to 'ennoble'

lives

with their 'perspectives'. Rembrandt, for example,
those terrific self-portraits—*pathos, self-knowledge . . . the rest.*
Dignity & failure—etcetera.   *Yes,*

but let fifteen minutes pass,
& he's having a banana.
Or is that me?

A rollmop, then.

Cath reads an old favourite, laughs occasionally,
reads me bits. The fan churns,
noisily. Tho we don't notice. The night cooling

after a day of 42 & another of 37. Cool tomorrow,
at 27? 24? A small list of things-to-do builds.
My first week back at work.

Write to Sal, draw my hand
or wrist-&-watch, stuff to edit, CDs to copy
for Michael. I recommend to him

Floyd Jones: 'Tore Your Playhouse Down'
how the song rolls so casually—solid, unfussed
the solos played on top of each other

a wonderful cacophony (Fred Below, Otis . . .)
The drawing—for Nick—illustration to something
he'll print. *Sal*——after 20 years—to be

evicted from her flat. A view I love. She must, too.
'Sydney'. Sydney as an idea. Slessor, Cossington-
Smith. Not that I care much about them: it is

Sal's harbour view suggests them.
At last someone wants to charge real rent.
(The old owners must have died?—or sold up?)

It will be weird if she moves somewhere I don't know.
West, I guess.

     A week later I have edited things,
Photocopied my arm—preparatory to drawing—
these are the easy things. Not written to Sal.

Tho what's to say? You have to say something of course.
Very likely she is ready for change. Regretting
the view she will lose—but impatient with the place

now the move is on. She was always something
of a Futurist. One pictures her beautiful, goggled head
hunched forward to the sights of a WWI Fokker,

or leaning low & forward on a 1930s motorbike. Laurie jokes
that I should send the T-shirts to Les Murray,
they are so big. On different sides of the planet

we smile at the idea of Les—wearing the Brainard
T-shirt, a graphic proclaiming a reading. For Ted Berrigan,
for Joe Brainard & Anne Waldman. ("Oh, boy!"

says Nancy on one, "a Poetry Reading!") Laurie's
new book is out. Fingers bent,
curled over, relaxed, I draw my left hand, held

palm upward, & the wrist. My plan is to get it right
then copy it quickly with a firmer pen
& add the watch-band. Nick requires an image

—with which to feature a particular
bright red—& a poem, against which the drawing will be
set. (A poem I wrote years ago—

that Nick found & likes. I like it, too,
so why not?)   Weeks have gone past. Unchanged, the world
continues—tho shifts occur, indeterminate. The

one stability is a US stalled, awaiting the appointment
of the next incumbent. Moves will begin
when he is sworn in—the slide, the counter-measures,

the moves of Russia, India, China, Europe.

Though it's been non-stop 'interesting times',
most of it, in my life, has been going on elsewhere,
a pointy end far from here. For me,

no military service, no economic disaster.
My luck runs out?
'Blues For The Girls', 'All Blues', 'Mary's Blues'—

names I consider

for a new book, 'Mary' being Mary Christie—
but it's also an early Coltrane tune—& really
I would like it dedicated to Cath & Anna, the women

in my real life. Mary,
an old friend—in India now—in *Japan* for
the last seven years. More. I lived in her house

in Westbury Street. *The Westbury Street Poems*—
once a title I hoped to publish.
I'm sitting here in Cork—the bar, not the town.

(Write to my Irish friends.) Joyce, or Joyce's father, was
pleased to have
a painting of Cork, painted on cork, apparently.

Amused, I guess, at the finality & nominal closure
of the pun:
What's that? 'Cork.'

I find most puns shit boring, but still more so
the declaredly learned—discoursing
on their own 'delight' in them,

as if puns were naughty, & daring, & confirmed
their membership of some club—a kind of unofficial
High Culture Mensa. By the same token, I hate intellectuals

going on about Sport.
Why am I talking of this?
I don't know.

So, here I sit in Cork, time running out, luck running out—
thinking about titles—tho I can't make up my mind, &
writing them down means I can forget again for a while—

& think about art criticism—*write* some at any rate.
That is what someone wants me to do. And I'm 'on to it'—
I tell them. (I've done the drawing, meanwhile, & sent it off—

my wrist & hand—looking not too deformed—tho not
resembling exactly mine—which could be *really* satisfying.
Like 'Cork'. *My own hand* by my own hand. Is that it?)

The letter to Sal is written, posted. I think it felt
too weird—shifty, dishonorable—to write here about
maybe writing—& then not get it done. I tell her

about my picture of her as a Futurist. The
close-helmeted figure, in goggles—coming from
a Lina Wertmuller film—tho which one? In it

the joke Fascist—lantern-jawed—dumb machismo type—
speeds about, aerodynamic—
acting out his picture of himself as he does.

Tho who am I to talk? (Not exactly lantern-jawed,

not exactly machismo—tho—like a Fascist—seemingly
a little down on intellectuals: *When I hear the word "pun"*
I reach for my revolver! Yike!)

Mimi The Metal-Worker.

My father's war—the second, 'world' war—was an odd one—
significant in his life—along the *Some Came Running* lines:
he was young, free (single, at least), he joined up

not to fight so much as to travel—
waiting for call-up would mean permanent duties
in Australia, & call-up seemed inevitable. My father

joined, hoping to see the world. He would have, too—
except he & his friend proved such a combination
on the 25 pounder the generals kept them home,

for permanent display. (See that tree on that hill,
says one general to another. I have a pair here
who can take it out first shot! Bolton! Nicholls! Load up!)

(Or so I imagine.)
Dad was stuck here
as his regiment—regi*ments*—would ship out . . .

to New Guinea, Africa, the Middle East. My father

took increasingly long vacations AWOL & was
regularly punished. *Why did you do this, Private Bolton?*
Because I could. *I see.* From that period of his life,

a kind of paradisal time of boredom, fun, cameraderie,
he had endless stories, that I heard endless times
& can remember & would like to hear again,

hear my father tell them. Tho he's gone. Time
having run out. (Me, my
watch, & I.)

Cath will show up soon, any minute, & we'll
cross the street & shop in the markets, buying
fruit & vegetables, bread—for the weekend & the Monday,

which is Australia Day & a public holiday.
(Public Holidays, unfortunately,
mean nothing to me—as *I don't work Mondays*—

& *nobody* cares about Australia Day—this is Australia!
Altho, increasingly, people seem to. Well, count *me* out.)

Whoa! Close call. The girl taking coffee outside
is nearly collected by a young guy on a skateboard going by.
Luckily she pauses on the doorstep just in time.

Cath's arrived. (Sal,
I was going to say, liked my father,
& his stories.) My time

would have been different—Vietnam.

(Which I am grateful to have missed. Demonstrating against it
was bad enough—the real thing would have been awful.
My father told me—I remember—not to go if I was called up:

'Disappear,' he said.

                              But it didn't eventuate.
It did for others.)

                    Australia Day,
at Margaret & Crab's. We sit out on their
verandah, in the dusk & then the dark, talking,

catching up, watching the street lights & moonlight
thru the leaves, listening to parties up & down,
watching young people visit. The dog, Molly,

excited & attentive, yapping occasionally,
at other times absorbed, silent.
It's hot, tho cool by now. Marg's hair,

cut shorter than usual—like a Cleopatra cut
but abbreviated, sharp. It resembles the haircuts of the girls
in Kirchner's & Heckel's paintings—& Schmidt-Rottluff's—

so severe & modern.

These models were the women Kirchner hung about with.
Girlfriends. I saw a photo of one recently—Nina Hardt—& was
Amazed at how modern the haircut seemed

Severe & sure, 'Bauhaus': the woman looked independent
& unfaked. Though this was *before* WWI—before
the Bauhaus, the Tingle-Tangle Girls, Dada.

It is a shock to see in the photo the real life
the painting depicted—suddenly actual,
a moment—not bent to a purpose.

Some of the Berlin scenes are pretty good.
But it's the scenes of bathing at the lake I like
& cabaret girls dancing—where Kirchner,

as well as being suckered by the women's beauty,
depicts their friendship & humour: in the chorus line
there are always two shown in conversation.

Crab points out the perfect sweetness & beauty,
& construction,
of a Little Walter solo behind Muddy.

Etta James is dead. I hadn't realized.

Perfect in her own way, a few times. An
unhappy life.

                    She will be remembered longer than me.
Unless, in the library, in the Himalayas, in 2333,
some monk decides the poetry of Australia 300 years earlier

really was interesting—& allows himself a footnote.
"Ken Bolton answered phones in an art gallery, ran a bookshop,
& wrote poems of wistful humour."

I see it in a small hand on an index card—
"a provincial poet in the era
of Late High Capitalism—

not much regarded,"

I have to laugh. What's that great line
of Apollinaire's,
about tossing your life off like a drink?

I finish my coffee up. (I expect
this looks like decision. Tho in fact it means
Time for work. I go there.)

AND WILLING, WILLING

my feet are going to get
cold but I forget them!
I am up early I am
up late, up
so early, anyway, it could
almost
be late

very much
the same thing,
don't you find—

you, who
are always
out there,
a-readin'?—

    I watch
the light,
till, like my feet,
I forget, play
a tape quietly
of Wayne Shorter
—*Ju Ju*— read:
poems of Frank O'Hara,
some of Meaghan—"mixity"
is that a word? why not "mix"?
now my feet are truly cold
as the house awakes—& I forget
again their fate,

which is a little bit
my fate —brrr—
           which is also
to *Make that toast, make that
tea,* & take them to you—
your cool face your warm feet—
hi

"HINDLEY STREET"

I write those words, the
title of this poem,
on this pad
to start a list—of things I must
do. Is this going to be a poem?
Isn't it?
        ("Hindley Street",
I know what it will mean.
Otherwise, names of people I should
email. Richard, in case
my silence is taken to mean something,
something dark, brooding— Micky, to break *her* silence.)
        Different
from what I had been
going to write—fired up
by the fetishized
nebulousness
of the Houynhhyms last night.
I get a haircut instead,
& with the head massage
that anxiety is syphoned off.
        Philosophers,
rub your heads!
        My hair
short again—my visage modern.
Now, to work—
to face down the future
as it comes on minute by minute—
incrementally, or like pirates boarding a ship,
storming on,

doing this & doing that—
me, not the pirates—
philosophy, meanwhile, simmers
on the back-burner. I add Simryn Gill
to the list. Hullo, Richard, Micky, Simryn!

"Doing this", or "doing that"
like a small-minded Frank O'Hara,
admittedly, a contradiction in terms

small-minded then, not like Frank O'Hara,
but with my haircut, at least—
ashamed of a century that is
ashamed of me, if it thinks about it.
Me, & the century—at neither of which
I can smile. Time to get
my head rubbed.

FACES AT NIGHT

it is late at night &, for the hell of it, I make
a tape, make cups of tea,
                         & the poets—the
poets I 'love'—
                   tonight they are "okay by
me".
          Where I sit
                  my image
                  faces me,
reflected in the dark of the windows opposite,
pleasantly blocked
                           —almost
entirely—
               by the window *frame*, so I don't
have to watch my face shift, endlessly, to
look alright,
               to get bored with, etc—

                                something,
tho,
          I may do later!
                           When you go
to write a poem, it is almost as if you must
choose—which sort of poet
                                you are
going to be.
                   For me it is like that—
sometimes.
                   For others, more authentic
than I, it may not be—

they have
something to be going on with, a vision to
reveal
continuously—
knowledge to
dispense—
not me.
"He's got
a nerve,"
a phrase always spoken in
my mind by a woman, an American—1947
to 1958—Eve Arden is my pick.
"Something
to be going on with" is said in simple-
minded triumph,
by an idiot who taught
me science,
after delivering something
primitive—
a slap across the head,
15
minutes more work, say, after the bell
—&, with those words, he shoots out
the door.
Not my head.
One of
the brighter ones, I was bright enough to
develop the earliest animosity to him,
amongst the students.
Baumgartner—all

is forgiven!
What else?
Now John, he sits
powerfully, at his desk, large shoulders
hunched, his mighty brain is finishing off a
line of powerful reasoning, & logic is
defied
—'stands' defied in fact—
or his
shoulders ('powerful') are *relaxed*, he pens
the opening lines—that roll easily, no
complication clouds (yet) their path
to mere description, tautology.
Tho it will.
They have already a smirk about them
these lines,
tho the face
('visage', 'dial')
that reflects this powerful brain, reflects it
oddly, the expression is one of puzzle,
slight consternation . . .
but that is John.

My face is reflected, but I can't see it.

Pam's
I can see—tho I see it from above, & it is in
profile, bent, having just paused, but bent
now
& writing quickly—two lines, three!

& she straightens. She is in her tiny study
at the bottom of the house—& I would
appear
          to have come down stairs, to see
her, & am *floating*
                    —to see her from this
angle—
          above the door—*near the transom!*
Is that what they are called—
                              the glass
window, or panel, above? (Again, I am
in a movie—black & white—that is how I
'see' the transom).
                    Who is on the other
side of that door,
          Ray Milland?

    or gangsters—unpacking one of those
large brown paper bags with lunch
in it?
      They are 'holed up' after a job—"the
hardest part is the waiting" (etc)
                              "I ordered
pickle!"
          What was Pam writing about?
She's finished now.
                    She sits back, fiddles
with a cassette-tape cover,
                    shakes it, to
see if it is empty,

                              but doesn't look to see
what tape it is.
                    She is thinking.
                                                    If it is
a good poem
                    I hope she sends it
                                            in the
mail.
          Then I can read it.

                                        The face of
Cath, when *she* writes—
                              I see it in profile,
as she sits at her desk, & as if I have just
entered the room—but am not, this time,
floating—
                    my head is about head high!
                                        Or
I see it
          as she sits in bed writing,
                                        & see it
full-on
          —tipped, tho, a little, toward the
plane
          of the paper she is writing on—her
face looks alert & intelligent, tho calm.
                                        I guess
apprehension is ruled out—& things are
getting done
                    Now I see the face

of Steve Kelen,

     large, dark, & brooding—
& suddenly Satanic

     now I see mine!

Because I have looked up, briefly
      —to wonder
has the record stopped, that I am taping?—
I resemble
   someone taking dictation—
the speaker has paused—the writing hand
stilled, head at attention.
       I am wearing a
jacket,
   an old suit jacket of grey, so I look
like a clerk—mid century—doing
stock-take—in a small-town country store.
       I look
slightly careworn, except there is almost
no detail
    —but if Edward Hopper were to
paint it, those are the details it would be
given, my dial—
     tho *"His painting days / are
over, son"* I hear the voice of . . .
       Forrest
Tucker
   (he of the Noble Visage & the career
high
    of season after season of

F Troop—not real big in my consciousness,
                                   tho I liked
it,
         another happy dystopia—like *Gilligan's*
Island or . . . what else? *Hogan's Heroes* — for
the 'Authoritarian Personality'. (Ah, thank you,
Frankfurt School!)
                                   I place my visage,
carefully, back behind the frame & continue
to write.
               Tho what to say?
                                   I wonder if
they have all written tonight?
                                   Steve, Cath,
Pam, John?

               The long face of Robert Gray,
Anna Couani—whose mother thought I
resembled a horse—the small, earnest face
of Jamie Grant
               (I've never seen it),
                                   the guy
who wrote *Ross's Poems*,
                    —(I wonder
         what
kind of face is Ross Bleckner's)—
                                   Laurie's,
looking
         Buddha-like yet careful.

A FRIEND OF HIS DAD'S

. . . he looks a bit beat
doesn't he, the wolf, there
in his suit, & stringy
loosened tie?

"Walter's first time
with *The Three Pigs,"*
I hear Helen tell Cath—
& *she doesn't want to frighten him*
As it happens
I'm first to read it.

He's pretty caught up in it,
so I give plenty of extra commentary.
"He's a tryer, isn't he, he doesn't give up.
What's he gonna do this time?"
Here's the
smart one of the
pigs again, getting up,
earlier & earlier,
to trick the wolf—

who must by this time
be getting pretty toey—

but these pigs
& this wolf
seem locked in to each
next step.
Narrative drive?

There's a photo
Peter sent—Walter,
looking pleased but confounded,
as the two walking fingers
of my hand march
across the table
towards him
as if to proclaim an ultimatum. It's
a year or so later now
& he still likes me
& I him. At best,
I will have a future
in his memory
that is almost fictive, a
'character' dimly remembered
—which is amusing
for me, now, as I
'be' that character,
knowing my attraction
is that I'm a friend of his dad's—
rendered therefore
'masculine'. The pigs,
meanwhile,
are in trouble,
& Walter knows it.

GUILTY OF STAYING UP ALL NIGHT

for Cath

Bernadette Mayer uses only first names:
I know who most of them are,
of course.
          (A 'New York' habit.
Maybe all readers should know who they are.
Maybe they will. One day.)

Now, Billy Moore & The Rhythm Aces
sing *Searching For My Love*
a terrific song, with a great,
muted sax line—repeated—quietly, yearning—
irresistible—you always want to sing it, tune
in
to the hold of the repetition.
Then Jan Bradley. She's great, too.
Mama Didn't Lie, she sings.
Bernadette Mayer is good on mothers.
Unsystematically.
It's not a last word on the subject
and better than you'd get if you set out
to have a 'last word'. The book is *Midwinter
Day*. I'm glad I'm reading it. It
didn't start out well, I thought. The
people are Ted (Berrigan), Lewis Warsh,
Clark Coolidge (Ron Padgett gets one mention,
where Bernadette figures he "doesn't trust" her),
Alice Notley. And Tom (who
may be Tom Clark)—other names whom
I don't know—one can only guess at—or they're
family or neighbours—early boyfriends, her sister,

friends from school, from memory, her parents
& the parents of others, *&*, intermittently, *everyone's* mothers:
hers, her friends'—& imagined mothers & occasionally
—which is almost peculiar to her, although
I know what she means—so maybe I think it too,
at some time, at some level—a perception of others,
including more men than women, a perception of others
as being a mother—as being even *her* mother. Or
composites of them (say, friend Ted, husband Lewis etc)
as "a mother". This seems to reflect a perception of them
as comforting, protective—and a need for them
to be that. Bernadette is herself a mother—
of 2 children—whom she watches closely, now.
The record has stopped. Dyke & the Blazers again?
—I mean Bobby Moore (& the Rhythm Aces). Hear it again?

Why not?
                    I sit for moments, contemplating
how tired I am & should I go to sleep & will Cath
be asleep at last—what position will I find her in
when I go to her room?—some nights she bops about a bit.

                    I put the record on &
                              wake up enough
to feel terrific, as well as tired, & pretend to be
one of the Famous Flames—on an easy gig—
(*Searching For My Love* is a slow song—I only need
to shuffle & repeat the one line: "Searchin, searchin,
for the one I love".) Then Jan Bradley sings again
as I sit down to write this. I sing with her, momentarily.

It is a controlled universe. The same record—same
Side—six times!
                        Searching For My Love is slow
& Jamaican sounding & a little like the riff from
Walk On the Wild Side—slower, & simpler, more
Pulsing—and it reminds me of a song called *"Guilty"*
—that is a favourite with a guilty person I know—someone who
    often
acts guiltily—which *I* find amusing. But it is a tender &
sentimental song—and humorous—&
probably represents
something of their softer side.
They heard it once, playing,
where I worked & asked after it
& got a copy. I hate feeling guilty. So do they, probably.
Who doesn't? The song says "Guilty—of loving you."
A terrific song. Time for bed.

IN JOHN'S ROOM

for John Jenkins

        Philip Guston
always makes me feel like a cigarette.
Every time.
        I have his *Smoking, 1*
1973, taped to my wall, a newspaper reproduction
torn, surrounded by the type, of
whatever article it once was, yellowing

in black and white
no wider than
the palm of my hand. The painting,

I see, is five feet square
from the photo I have, now, of it — Guston sitting
in front and to the side.
                The poet — test-flying
the new emotions, the new subjectivity. Most
likely — that is, 'most nights' — I sit in my room
reading — and reading over old notes, the notes
of last week, of last year, and picking up things
here and there, and reading them, thinking. And start
a poem occasionally. I love those movies of
        test-pilots,
the mad scenes where the others wait for
the plane to appear, reappear, return, or watch it
dive, the pilot's little struggling head, scarf blowing —
if it is an open cockpit — a little blood, maybe, appears
at the corner of his mouth. Down below
much wringing of hands. Most often
you don't finish the poem, you reappear

walking slowly, helmet in your hand
like the Grand Prix driver who's crashed somewhere
on the other side of the track, or stalled, and walks back
to the pits

          A Sailor's Life. John and I
laugh about it : sailors confined to ship—
for the storm to blow over, or somehow becalmed.
There they are, burping and farting, writing letters
bunks all around, Play us a song, Scottie,
pinching someone's picture of a loved one
and running about with it, all in shorts and t-shirts
someone obsessively clipping their moustache, or the hair
in their nostrils, Why do you do that Tony?
Boy, one of them says, *if I could only get a date*
with her! — of a female voice on the radio. Playing cards.
Where's Frank? Frank, what are you *doing?* Nuthin',
says Frank
              In the cockpit of today's new poem,
to quote John, things are different — the same record
or tape is on, playing softly, a bright desk lamp
is almost punishing in its brightness, every light
in the room is on, the heater — if it is winter — is blowing.
A drink, a cigarette, a coffee.
                After all these years,
the artist says — not me, an older artist (Philip
Guston?) — *I still don't know how it works* —
and chuckles. What I hate, about those quotes,
the self-congratulating mystification.
                  It is all, actually, an
exercise—

to make one bearable to oneself, or forgotten.
"WELL, WHO CARES, BUD — if this is all
'preliminary'?"

                    Right.   (My body,
I notice, is rocking, slightly, back and forth
to a tape I have rocked back and forth to
for ages — more than ten years. I spend
so much time by myself
      it is a wonder
I can bear the company of any other one. Is
this the new subjectivism (if not 'subjectivity')?
I look now at the horrible (cheerful,
ugly) bearded garden gnome
that sits on John's studio desk
two feet from me, holding
a football, one hand on its hip, dressed in team colours.
John has hung a roll of masking tape
over its pointed head, at a rakish angle.
(It's an early Xmas present for an in-law
of Shan's, Shan with whom John lives.) It looks arrogant
and comically aggressive — as though just awarded
a penalty. Its uniform is blue
with red and white : short-sleeve shirt and short pants,
on its head a pointed blue beanie : white hair
white beard, pink face and fat pink legs
little bright eyes. Its smile is matter-of-fact, certainly.
                            Now

Nancy Wilson sings *This Bitter Earth.*
                  Kind of thing I love.

IT'S COME TO THIS

I have become
The sort of silly bugger

Who eats alone
In a restaurant full of young people

Drinks

And reads a poem
And then another

Written by Larry Fagin
Tonight
25 years ago

IN TWO PARTS (ENLISTING WITH THE MODERNS)

for John Forbes

Ted's *one, two, three* —
"The Art of The Sonnet —
for Tom Clark"

teaches many people nothing.
Teaches me
what Ted teaches always—

why cannot
that lesson
be stamped indelibly

in my heart
& I, invincible,
rise womanly—
& slop oatmeal

on the referee
who would give a
points decision

to some leading stooge,

while I, I rage
at a brown desk,
in a blue jumper, 'knocking'

my head—against
the brick wall

that is my ambition? Hunh?

Ambition! *I never knew ye*—
you
you-you-you,

nut, you!

For I have
the *key* to that wall,
to the door *in* it,

to the Secret Garden

a maze, where—nutty, yes,
but beautifully—
Bud & Lou watch out

for the ghost, the ghoul—
for Frankenstein,
for the trap door—

for *the girl*—in short, fitted skirt,
knees & feet together
who holds a small purse

before her private 'parts'.

•

Thunder rolls across the sky
—which is "darkling".
I *guess* that is what that is.—

& a little god runs in,
leaping streams & hedges,
from the rather "Poussinesque"

landscape

out of the rain

& shares the gazebo with Bud & me
—realists of the old school
it turns out:

it is *Lou* searches in the rain—
for the girl—

(an umbrella that won't work
for comedy, prophylactics
for the old *joy! joy! joy!*

"perverted acts in pastures"
love).

I see him now
trading punches, haymakers,
but landing many blows,

leaninginto his quarry—

his trunks high, his
little sweating torso
merely pallid—

where the target,

an armless, legless, plinth-bound
statue,
is truly white.

This is the last round,

this must be an all out effort—
on the plinth the name
Boring Dud

chiselled

in Times Roman,
& a little poem by
Robert Gray.

LOUNGE ROOM

           Nothing's going
to come of this.   I sit, staring, at a
Xmas tree.

         The hum of the fridge.
      Glossy,
            black reflection —
of the kitchen—in the windows
               — *just*
north north west—
         not quite dead ahead.
       (To my right slightly.)
Grains
      picked from the tablecloth—
to chew.
      In the spirit
           of Primo Levi (!)
though with much less import
             consider
my non usage of the word
           "vulgar"
among other things.
      Is this thinking?
(basically:
      its use claims an entitlement),
. . . having read the poems of a friend
& the badly slipping mind
           of one of our
senior poets
     (that is, I have read his poems, too.
     I *haven't* read his mind).

*

I have described everything in this scene before,
                    from two different directions

                    *

My mind whirs in neutral—
                    idling 'high', but idling.
Red-checked tablecloth,
                    the chair opposite—
a pumpkin lounge,
                    (two cushions on it that are,
                                        I guess,
'bisque')
          backed against the black glass;
                              fish in emerald tank;
              CDs;
                    a twenty year old TV;
now
          — (I've never looked
                              this far right before,
in a poem) —
                this will sound arty:
                              a print of frescoed
city-scape—clay brick colours,
                    shaley, grey green sky
                    above it

                                              —a detail
                              of some Piero della Francesca—

thin, shiny black frame.
To either side below, standing guard, two little figures—
the Martian centurion from the Bugs Bunny cartoons—
one looking 'mad'
                              (angry), the other 'supplicant'.
That's about
              as far right as I can go,
                                        without looking
                                          'back',
over my shoulder.
                              If I do that
I see:
              the flue of the wood heater—
                                        a polished metal tube
ascending into the ceiling—
                              & the door
                                        —closed—
to the hall, down which
                              are the bedrooms, where
the others are sleeping:
                              Cath,
                                        Anna,
                                                  whose
homework
              sits open here
                              on the table,   & Gabe,
usually either 'out' dancing
                        ('elsewhere')

                              or here,
to my left, on the phone—but left is another story.

crowded buildings—tiled roofs, tiny windows
roofs peaked, spired, castellated: walls mostly,
planes—looking *trecento* rather than
Renaissance, but in effect more hermetic-period Cubist
The right wall is cinnamon coloured.
                              Below the
picture—& what the Martians stand on—is
a sideboard, dully polished wood, a small
mirror in it that has a lot of gleam, a detail amongst
the casual mess—of vase, cassettes, envelopes,
long lost school circulars, & biros, pens
                                        that litter it
                                        "temporarily".

                    Anna sits
                              before the TV
young   bored
                entertained   taking it in
                              but I hope
not too poisoned
                    she is critical very interestingly,
often.
                    The programs she likes have merit
tho basically
                    we don't watch it: Cath watches
The Simpsons with her
                              & I watch *Seinfeld*.
Gabe channel hops mostly—as does Anna when it

dips too low. I watch Cath's English (I.E., British) programs
with her on the weekend,

>   but Anna then is not here.
Does our not watching have much effect?—

>   some, I guess.
Imprinted is the model of Cath's reading,

>   which she does
constantly,

>   which Anna does more & more. Conventional worries,
these, I recognize—amounting to

>   "fingers crossed".
>   Cath says

>   the *chair*, not the pillows,
is bisque,

>   & the pillows I suppose
would be russet-ochre.

>   My idea of bisque is
packet-soup lobster

>   —a girl's (a woman's) idea
of an abomination typical of a bachelor—& it *is* years
since I made it, 20 maybe. Probably the Yangtze

>   (the
Yellow River)

>   is the colour of the lounge chair.

>   My art-historical education
had not prepared me for the fragments of Piero

>   when I saw them.

>   Tho they *were*
>   very fragmentary.

(The stuff in the Louvre was great.

                        Not just Piero—
everything!)
            I remember better

                   & liked
almost unaccountably—
                the main street of Arezzo—
as viewed from our hotel window
at night—
            just because I was happy probably.
Our trip to Europe.
             One small
                  all-night pizzeria:
its fluoro on the blink
               & some colourful characters
calling in, unable to sleep, hanging about.
                The beautiful
moist cool air. Hot at first—& then it rained.
              Cath put Piero up there—
        replacing a too bright—
because not correspondingly good—
          sub Stuart Davis thing.
          Actually
I don't have too much art, capital 'A',
around me, in my own room:
        a Brainard *Nancy*,
a little Micky Allan—
        of a goalie
happily missing (by a mile) his 'save',
           things

I've drawn
  —pictures of friends mostly—
        & a few
photocopies
    (like the Brainard), or things from magazines—
a photo of Benjamin's (non) burial place, women
sweeping up the bombed Reichstag in 1945, some
striking matchsellers (girls 8 to 18) in England
in Disraeli's time, an Ian Abdulla scene
& a Linda Marrinon. Politics & irony, mostly.
No room—to put up the Boucher I used to have up
(& must still have, somewhere)—
       that also seemed
to me
  ironic:
     Diana pursued by wolf, who expires,
having an arrow thru his head, but as if from the effects
of a Micky Finn.
      And all the Manet, Matisse, Dufy etc —
stuff I love—who wants to be surrounded
by flower pieces? I love it, but
    "The Refinement! The Refinement!"
I love it,
    but to live with it I would be ashamed.
    Perhaps wrongly.
       But there it is.
     #
I 'work' at a Contemporary Art Space.
     #
     This room—

Cath's victory
            against politics, defeat,
                        material want.
It is contingent,
            but kept up—
                        & in it the world is mediated,
discussed (TV, mail,
                  dinners are served,
                              moods, comforts,
favours, complaints
frictions   love   are
                        doled out, met with,
placed, sifted, arraigned, tempered,
                        borne
a locus of values:
                  from Anna's early morning—
a 12 year old getting quietly up,
                        doing some flute practice or
watching TV, getting
                        a snack together for school;
to me
      alone, up at night;
                        & dinners in between—
& Cath
        reading on the lounge
                        in the daylight she loves
—from here filtered thru the green of leaves, vines, distant trees,
the nearby lemon tree—the fish—moving languidly.

MY FATHER

I walk out on the pier
& in the dark the boats are each
a grey-white shape
facing into the wind. Slapping noises
come from them,
or more often a thud,
—water lapping at their hulls—
the sibilance carried away
in the wind.
Unattributable to any
one boat, the sound lulls —
forgotten. There are
lights on the shore—
& from the few fluoros
on the pier itself
the water appears to move past
in mysterious, diaphanous, greeny
greys—moody—black-&-
white movieish. Further over the sea
is John Jenkins—a postcard tells me—
in India. How? Why? I sometimes
think of him wearing white,
tho I think it was 15 years ago
that John regularly
dressed that way. Cath is beside
me, beneath the red eiderdown. Pam
is in Sydney, Laurie in New York. The room
in the little holiday shack is brown. Beachport.
Gaby & Yuri are playing cards, Anna
sleeps in the room in between. My dad rages,

lonely & demented—in Sydney
where I grew up, & left him,
& return, in a few days.

EARLIER

coffee's on the stove
coming on,

Cath away—trying for
tonight's squid—

vegetables spitting
as they roast in the oven.

#
there's the coffee now.
#

I fool about with
pen & paper
the scene from
fishing this arvo:
trees on the left
above a white
Vee-dub—
back to us,
its boot open—
water beyond. Like
a cover scene for a
Nordic novel: the abandoned
car signalling death or 'peril'—
though further right the
rocks run out, to the tiny
jetty, its legs leaning,
grouped together, in

a way that suggests
brushed, Japanese characters

—inked brush-strokes—

stubby verticals,

rippling water
before & behind,

a scene
that plays out rightwards
as the jetty extends
     . . . into a bay
that curves round
further on the right.

Endless sky, of
grey, silvery cloud, above.
    Cath & some guy & his
grandson, holding lines, in
parkas & hoodies & shapeless clothes.

Australia & the familiar.
The genre-less every-day. A
holiday day,
               of pressurelessness
& of time passing
of cloud & sky . . .
      & the 'verities',

of the simple
Japanese construction—the
stabbed, brushed
verticals & horizontals—
the line cast

THINGS TO DO ON THE ISLAND

                     great title—
In the very easy sense—
               where you
say that sort of thing
               (Great)
                     —(is it?
Really?)
          anyway—it *IS* what's
               on
my mind:
          (THINGS TO DO)
               READ THESE POEMS,
IN THIS NEW BOOK
          'this'?

which new book, whose?

                  why in fact
these questions—
             of myself—when
I am writing the poem,
               aren't I?
        because I'd like
        to *like* them
        & *report* I like them—

but am not sure that I do or that I will
               #
          those poems
               #

So . . .

        read them.

                Stop talking
to myself, too, maybe.

          & there's
'Do the drawings'—

        to accompany Greg's stuff—
do

    a picture *of the view*

        from Gabe & Stace's
          kitchen,

their last one, in London—

            from memory,
but

  —if not—

      from this photocopy—

        a view I loved,

      but maybe not
      loved by them

it reminded probably of going to work,

            of
how small the flat was,

      relatively,

            of

London routine

    (a railway line,

        a noisy train

at regular intervals)
                          —the
                    day to day—

                    but I loved it.
                                        Draw that.

All I have to do really. It won't matter much
if I don't do any of it.
                          There will always be
a new book of poems.
                    Greg's poems
                                        I will
illustrate,
            or decorate   —   or I won't
                                        & it
won't matter.
                    The London drawing
                                        I can make
on the light-box
                    from a photocopy—

                                        (trace, add
charcoal.
            I might
                    'love' doing it—I usually do)—
some late night,
                    at home,   some time.

                    Nothing else.

                                        So,
nothing much to do

I read the Murnane book I found in the library—
                                        & it's terrific.
Write a poem about insects,
                              sitting in the sun
                                              near the
'what-bug-is-that' poster.

                        Towels on the line very still.

Birds move about. Cath, I think, fishing.

"HI, SMALL BUG!"

*"Hi, small bug, I'm not grass—but climb me. It's
me, by the way, Issa!"*

That sort of thing.
                How many bugs have I dealt with
down here?
          (A few spiders
               I've killed.)
                          A scorpion
                                &
an insect
        I've *helped move*
                    —from the sliding door
                      frame
to outside—
          the cement step, the garden.

I have spent a lot of time
                    perusing the *poster*
—*BUGS OF OUR TIME* ? —

                  flightless insects,
primitive-winged insects, water insects etcetera
their fanciful names:
             chalcyd wasp,
                      water penny,
the true midge
        (a false midge, by implication, exists—
               the pseudo midge ?)

        #

My oldest friends, a meeting after forty years—
how will it go, how *might* it go?

                                    Or, since it will

—we meet on Sunday—

                           it will, but *how?*

#

                                   Ichneumon wasp

damsel fly

the (plain) water beetle
whose rummy cheerful

look I like

the emperor (or 'gum') moth

& I think "Gotha"—
a German aeroplane?—
"Genghis"—a conqueror?

#

I read some more Patrick Leigh Fermor

#

An exhausting day
of driving up & down the coast,

70

we do in fact rise suddenly & say
"We have to go!" tho our hosts

are not startled

familiar with the concept "the last ferry":

#

I consider these bugs again,

as I am
'here', again, now.

They *can* read
as a lesson—an illustration
of *orders* & *kinds* of life

(different 'stations' etc)

Leigh Fermor
mentions "mooch" & I wonder

when "mooching about" became
a regularly used phrase.
'Moose the
Mooche' I think at the same time.

But I am not mooching—

This is a small house.
I sit
        —very still—

by the sliding door, in the light

—fly-screen between me & the green outside . . .
. . . where the real bugs are

a moment later I test that phrase,
hear it in Penny's voice,

see Alex glance outside, smile.
As I would smile if Penny said it.

(LATE AT NIGHT, BRUNY ISLAND)

            here
in the bookshelves of the
holiday house is a book of
John's poems—also
Les—a fat spine
appropriately.
Why is that here?
Masochism?
I am unlikely to read it.
Anyway,
I wonder what John's got to say—
this time.

         *

        Across
the table from me
my jacket is draped over the chair,
reminding me a little of John—
a presence *and* an absence. It
looks more like what he would wear
than I would—& it's empty,
no one there.
Undoubtedly it's mine.
              Why write
so often about John Forbes? I knew him
only so well.
        To rise
to some
     test—
    or 'occasion', yes?
(No?) (Maybe?)

                    The radio—
ABC from Hobart—
is playing: very good music
that I don't know—
in the adjoining room, so it's
both on but ignored
easily enough,
                    as if I'm
alone more or less—
opposite the chair & jacket,
looking at it, but sometimes
at the things between us on the table
a thin-striped table cloth, blue &
white—pens pencils salt & pepper shakers—
books—that Cath & I are reading—
a yellow Spirax notebook
A-5, a small stub of candle . . .
a tape measure,
black & yellow—black, with some yellow
    detailing.
Stuff.
            The light is mounted
behind me, on the wall,
rather than above:
the room lit like a bar
or cantina—& they are those sort
of doors opposite, too—
bar-room half-doors, open,
leading into the middle space
(& the radio).

Low ceiling, stucco walls, an earthen
nougat-magenta.
                              The shelves—
the book shelves—
since I began with them,
are on my left, at
the far end of the room.

This is not the sort of poem
John would write.
He would not see the point.
And in fact I don't see the point
as yet, tho I may hope to find one.

Christ knows where.
                              The
news is on now, following
cricket-all-day.
A decade ended, of
Kerry O'Keefe's commentary—
his wheezy laugh, his humour—
to which
I never attended. (John might have.
But no, gone too long.)

                              I always
try to write something
when I'm down here.
                              Start
& wait & see where they go. John chimes

with the cricket—& maybe with
the saloon-bar doors—but otherwise
he is a bit urban
to gel with the island—
& holidays. Or is that just
John-as-I-conceive-him?
The book is on the shelf tho.
That is a fact.
                    I look at the poems,
'Love Poem', 'Night Shift',
'History of Nostalgia'

          working from the back:

                          " . . . attitude
is the poems' currency, an asset
only when it is spent" it says
on the cover. I wonder if John
wrote that copy.

                    I wonder
where I am going with this?
A long time trying to locate an attitude,
      or summon one—like someone scowling,
      or non-committal, leaning against a wall
      (near a corrugated iron water tank—*as* I
      envisage it—now—tho how or why?)

who pushes himself off, finally, with
some resolve

                        (spits in the grass?)
            throws smoke away / spits in grass
Tho this is uncharacteristically—of me—
not quite urban,
                        & Australian, tho
I 'am' an Australian.

        Like 24 million other people

                —is *that* my attitude?—

more or less the same, more or less different; up late
in my case; trying to write poetry

POEM (NEW WAY OF WORRYING)

for Sal & Pam, Jenny Layther, & Neil Paech

Here I am in the coffee shop
I look at my list of things
to do. But which
to start on? Jen
comes in, orders—
dressed in many layers
of black—like someone
out of Daumier.
A beautiful
young
Japanese woman
goes past,
(short skirt,
pale-stockinged legs)
in boots, & white, woolly coat—
holding a coffee—(legs
she wishes maybe
were slenderer—
but she'd be wrong)
talking happily
to a guy as she walks,
a taller, Aussie male.
So does she worry?
I haven't seen Neil
for ages. *Should* I *worry—
about him?* I haven't thought
of him in ages, either.
I worry, really, about
Pam, Sal,
me & Cath.

                    The young Alison Currie
goes past. I worry maybe
about others as a way
of worrying about myself,
or disguising that I do.
Do I worry
because I'm *bored*? The
terribly handsome, terribly
continental-looking guy at
the table nearby is on the phone
—very Australian voice—
like a hitman
in a Wim Wenders movie—
Jean-Louis Trintignant—
who started
out, I think,
as a formula one driver
a name I knew as a kid—
then drove one of the cars
in a famous movie—
& moved into film
soon after. (Soon after,
I moved into poetry.)
                    The Italian-looking
guy—Jean-Louis
was French—has gone,
I see now, &
the guy he was with,
who looks more like
'the muscle' in

any good movie kill,
is pushing out
the door—where Jen
is sitting, in the fresh air
looking at papers,
mind on the job.
I feel the air
on *my* skin, imaginatively.
Yes, I could be
out there, too.
But here I am
in my regular spot,
worrying.
Now Jen moves off
wrapping
her cloaks about her—
an elegant
rag-picker (Manet),
an antiquarian
(Honoré Daumier)—
& my friend, Terry, arrives—
acquaintance really. We nod.
So, Pam, how's it going?

RE PETER BLACK

Dear Greg,
          I expected to be writing this
up late
        surrounded by books, music playing quietly,
having a bit of a think
               I think I thought
I'd think about
           Peter Black and Robert Frank,
about the darkness
            that seems to be at the centre
of a lot of New Zealand art
               or seems somewhere
to haunt it
        & figured I'd have trouble
                  separating this
from the literal darkness
           especially as the latter
signals the former most often — or is there in its stead.
As a literalist
       which for the most part I am
                  it is
the literal darkness I see most
           — see *only,*
tho I intuit occasionally
         that it is
              symptomatic
of something else.
      I was going to make some comparisons
of New Zealand & Australian attitudes
          to this

                              'metaphysical dark'
Tho "metaphysical"
                    I never have
                              a firm handle
on it —
          a bit Spiritual   & a bit
                              Ontological,
is that it?
              where the bodies go wobbly & out-of-phase
on *Star Trek* or
              The Outer Limits,   indicating some
redistribution of particles
                    thru a wooze-machine
to another time, or form?
                    Uri Geller —
is that metaphysical?
                    This invites being
                              written off
as a lightweight, I know.   I'll stop.
                              The
thing I was going to suggest
                    was   —
                              the
New Zealander's quieter,
                    greater confidence
                                        stems
from facing this darkness more directly. Australians
it's often held are nervous of the empty interior —
to which we keep our backs. Inverted commas
come in here flocking to save the words from bald

assertion, naivety —
                    I.e., held by whom,   not
Me
      then there's "empty"   —   it's not 'empty'
                                        & who
believes this anyway?   I never think about
the dark, empty, arid interior.
                              But then, is there
an Australian more nervous?
                              And it's true
                                        ("true" —
can you say that?)   —   Australians worry about who
they are
            New Zealanders seem quite sure
                                        Tho
our art seems sunnier
                  — disposition-wise.
                                        Yet
New Zealanders
            do daggy better —
                                    a kind of recognition
of the dark abyss
                  thru laughing at it ?
                                    In Melbourne
our daggy merely 'forgives' the inevitable failure of
everything . . . to live up to its pretensions.
                                    Not so dark
you see.
            So we have Tony Tuckson:
                                    you have McCahon

we have Bill Henson, you have
                              Peter Black.
I prefer Tuckson & Black
                         McCahon seems always
more 'Steptoe' than 'Beckett'
                         Henson   too obvious
in the pathos & the Beauty
                         — he 'quotes' them, sure —
                              a cake he'd
like to have *and* eat
                         "have" as if he
didn't care, "eat" as if shielded by irony . . .
                                   Incriminatin'
is partly its business
                    — as if to feel dirty were to feel modern.

Take Black's dog-at-night in the back seat of the car,
the peacock in the park,
                         the politician on election night
amid balloons — the narcissus seal.
                                   I like all these
& liking, responding to them,
                         seems the point.
                                        A
Henson photograph's point is our thinking, our unease
about our response.
                    Black's work might be from an
earlier era
            which is the way — or is why —
                                   the comparisons

84

with Robert Frank's *The Americans.*
The first morning

I've had free
to write like this

I'm not up late, Greg —
it's

just past 10 a.m.
in a coffee shop in Hindley Street

(Adelaide)
the waitress wears no lipstick this morning

but otherwise it's exactly where I always am,
looking

at some older Italian guys rabbiting on at a table outside
(I look thru the glass — the radio is on, coming
from a speaker above my head — a girlie voice singing —
bright sun, traffic outside,
bright gleam,
from a metal

rail outside &, much brighter, light bouncing off a car
over the road. I look up
to confirm there's nothing
interesting

to say about it
other than that it's black —

(the car)
& it's gone.

Another Richard Estes morning
that only I have

in Adelaide
because I think that way

                                        yes, I, only I!
And that's 'daggy' Adelaide-style.

                              We can dream
(of being cosmopolitan)

                    but we can't *be* (cosmopolitan).

                                        The failure thesis
once again

                  (tho I had it first only a moment ago —
do I really believe in this?)

                        It is probably easier in Wellington
to be confident of your place in the world.

                                        Why?

                                                Don't ask:
more geography rings you about

                              you remember constantly
two islands, north & south, *volcanoes,*

                          shipping,

                                        & the clouds

roll by overhead

                  as if *reeled.*

                        You think, "edge of the
world"

            & *there's* the darkness

                                  plus the fierce presbyterian
puritanism.

                  Dark enough for you?

                                    The photographs seem
symmetrical, balanced

                    — the monkey-with-the-camera, the woman
lying in the park, the nun (her gesture,
                                        the cross
below her face),
                    the Maori biker gang —
                                            which says
look at this
                    evidence, things captured, glimpsed
but too artlessly to have remembered to 'look' artless.
                                The bunny garden-gnome,
the seal,
            joking recognition   of the 'human condition'
: pathos, 'suffering'
                        & the way animals — like cartoons —
                                            illustrate it
So we get to have our pity
                            but not expend it —
                                because these are jokes.
& on the woman politician, the woman asleep on the grass
we expend a more real, & realistic, recognition —
of the human
                    — in specifics: not an allusion (the seal's
Narcissism, the dog's beseeching))
                                Carol Jerrems
makes a contrast
                        an Australian photographer
                                                more
concerned with the relations *between* people
                                    in her photographs.
Robert Frank's America was more various

                                        than New Zealand
far more diverse — & tense *with* it —
                                    less cohesive
                                                    more
policed & coded
                        micro-managed
                                        Peter Black's Maori bikers
is not a Robert Frank picture
                                less bizarre
                                        less alienated
pictures New Zealand can assent to
                                    the way America could not
to Robert Frank's.
                            The more limited truths, the
depth & singularity of New Zealand.
                                        All the stuff
I didn't want to find I'd said.
                                Photographs are great
the way they raise up all that is irrelevant—or
                                                    not
quite the point, about them—
                            & *they* remain,

                                                    you
hold them in your hand
                            but you can't put
your finger on it.

SALUTE

I wonder what happens
in Seb's kitchen, I see
him round the corner
into the room, sun shining, cat
ready for food, a grin
that is mixed of resignation
& amusement eyes alight
for the opportunity
each day brings. I always
liked the way he understood
things—things I've
never understood—
as an open secret, knowledge
with which he nudged me
forward. He faces, I guess,
a beach view, opens orange juice
or sets coffee up
hits the surf? He might. I
never did. In fact, Seb's
gaze said *Hi, I'm me you're*
you I know what I'm
going to do for the day,
what about you? amused
at my life
—the comedy of error—
pleased that I managed it.
I'll put a record on, Seb, like
I always used to—today
one you'd recognize *Velvet Underground*
live 1969 or Coltrane's *Giant Steps*

but in the functional way you
would do—*the necessary steps*—fix
juice, move the cat off the chair, check
the surf. You?

SANCTUARY

I see a woman get out of a car
                              Briefcase in hand
Hurriedly &
                    Leap to the footpath!
                                        Here comes
The Ezra Poundy-looking guy
                              shuffle shuffle
Negotiates step,
                    Waves as if nonchalantly
                                        To his pal
Always well-dressed, the pal,
                              like a French or Italian politician
The other Italian guys
                    — at the table outside:
                                        Discussing,
Laughing
          — While I begin my poem on 'Europe'

& take notes
              on European history
                    for the Banana's assignment.
Europe, get out of my mind!
                              But who else
Do I relate to?
              Who can think about
              the USA — the Madness
              Of King George (the younger) ?
                    Bush, Bush the second.
                                        Depicted
So often

as a chimp
    Exactly as I think of our
        own
       glorious leader —

   Howard

  #
  irony?
  #

    A bunch of crooks
       Last week's essay was
          WWII
marked liberalism's failure?
        Across the road
The major domo, or doorman,
       in resplendent uniform
Moves, *& looks*, amusingly, like Benny Hill.
         Finally
The taxi driver to whom he talks
       (thru the glass
        I see only
Hill's signature beaming face
      Vast tummy in suit
Epaulettes.
    Rising
    on the balls of his feet,
       pleased with himself)
the taxi driver gets out, a small guy,

                                        & is eating
an enormous,
fully-peeled banana
                        small & bald.

                                              Now
                                              the
                                              smaller, bald
                                              Midget
Who runs the tattoo shop
                              Rockets by.   I'm surrounded
                                            by nuts

I wonder who I look like?
                              Hate to think.
                                                    That is,
I'd hate, probably, how I *do* look.
                                        Hindley Street —
A smallish, muscular young guy swaggers past across the street,
Striped black-&-yellow shirt,
                              cigarette smoked with a
                                        swagger, too
Everyone a caricature.
                                        Yesterday, walking beside,
I hear ". . . that's what they did you see. That's how they
                                        Fucked up.
They weren't using radio waves." He has a friendly, doleful
                                                    Face
                  looking straight ahead
& we're side by side, at the lights. "What *were* they using?"
                                        I ask.

                          93

"Wires," he replies, "And the satellites should have had
                                        circuit-breakers."
"What, wires in space?" I ask, incredulous—"They had
them wired to each other, these satellites?"
He thinks for a moment. "Yep." He goes on.
"Must've looked pretty funny," I suggest, but
he's okay-with-that
                              & we part.
The morning route.
                        That morning, I ducked in
& got the mail from the post office
                              Today I
Already have it
              & get to work —
                              & from inside
I push up the roller door
                        to find Julie Lawton
On the other side
                        poised like Charles Atlas
A Charles Atlas who's just done a clean & jerk
One foot well back, the other leg forward
Bent at the knee — arms in the air, a 'Vee'
Of load-bearing triumph.
                        In no *other* way
                              evidently crazy.
I smile.

STARTING NEAR THE CAKESHOP

                    A young
Islamic woman,
Turkish
ambles slowly
towards me, & past,
chewing gum,

so slow
she almost
moon-walks, a

flash of white
as the bubble
swells & bursts.

                    I sit
in the car
passenger side
while Cath goes
for pasties.

And another,
of some dumber
sect, shuffles
neurotically past—

dreadful frock,
veil on her curls,
harried, hunched
cast to her shoulders.

Cath returns.
Did I see
the nutter one? The
fundamentalist? Yes.
And that the Turkish girl
was blowing gum?
Yes. Both
pregnant, says Cath.

I pity the child
of the nutty one, the
severe, tense, curious
life it will have, till with
luck it rejects them

The nutter—lost to the
system she has
embraced, defeated
sufficiently
that its regimen
confirms her view—
life is hard.

          Sick,
I am relaxed enough—
like the Turkish girl,
a babushka in
layered rags &
head-scarf
soaking up the sun.

                    Earlier,
with Clinton, age 3, &
Marg, his mum—Cath's
sister—Marg said
Clinton, what is *that?*
of a child's whistle
he'd picked
from the opportunity
shop. "Take it back or
pay her for it—
before she has a
breakdown."

A little harsh.
         I guess the woman
has been eyeing
them, too.

For myself I figured OK,
I'm a guy,
in a large black coat, down at
heel: "She's suspicious,
fair enough."

                    She had watched
me play idly
with a Rubik's Cube
Clinton handed me,
watched me, I thought,
pityingly.

Later
to come bursting forth—
while I sat against
the bonnet of
the car—demanding
to know where I'd put
it.
　　　As I moved
to show her, towards
the shop, she darted
in. She obviously thought
I had it
secreted
in my pocket. Poor
woman.
　　　　　Made a halfwit
by Life—and only
my age—
　　　　　dressed in a
horrible
ribbed wool
pantsuit of green
and orange.
　　　　　Cath &
Marg
　　　are efficient
full of life, checking things
while Clinton & I
hang around outside

he blowing his whistle,
in answer, each time,
to a dog who barks opposite—

till it becomes apparent
there are *two* dogs . . . &
how to answer them?

Cath I remember
wrote a poem about
Op Shop women, the
horror of certain kinds

"He's got a whistle
would a dollar be alright?"

(Marg)
or that is the exchange
I saw, I didn't hear
exactly—as the woman
hovered
at the door.
                    It is June 15,
bright weak sun
warm air that will chill soon,
the bark of all the trees
dark with the night's rain.

Goodbye Marg,
Goodbye Clinton.

                    Cath
drives me home, where
I will get well,
                    sleep
& read. I wake
when Michele arrives
with—
          oddly enough
(though typical) a
dress for Cath, a
very good one, from an
Oppy she says "& think
yourself *lucky* because
I could almost get
in it."

          I sleep, listening
to them talk in the
room down the hall.

TRANSPORT / TRAIN RIDE

                    Anna's car radio:
voices babbling away—
a professionally dumb
breakfast trio ("Dumb

is democratic, right?"
"Actually,

Don't Waste My Time.")
                 after a moment
I sing to myself   I'll /
be seeing you
but tho I love that song
I only know

a joke version: *At the bar /*
& at the races, come what may
do doot-doot doo etc I sing it softly
Anna
is not listening to the drivel
But she did put it on
Might be rude
to sing over it.

             As we
whip thru town—which is
exciting, she's a good driver—
the morning traffic
is alert & competitive
not yet in grid-lock:

(WE'RE ALL GOING
TO BE EARLY!)

the sky is early-winter clear—
An adventitious red light
means I can jump out

quite close to work
I do & when I get there

there's an email
from Pam: her poem—

a train trip.
It's a good'un

The only other train-trip
poem I know is Berrigan's.
His tho
is not a commute

but a trip home
from a holiday:

standard issue people with
food crumbs all over them—
noting each other, making themselves
at home, striking up
conversations.
Pam's has the

commuter rhythm.
(I must know others:
New Yorkers—
always training off
to the Hamptons

or somewhere.) In Pam's poem
she passes Sasha
in Rookwood, the cemetery—typically,
     they're arguing.
An argument with Sasha
was a pointless thing—

about the things
I cared about—

his views weren't mine,
or even interesting,

though he was. His politics
I liked. I didn't
know him well.
Pam's poem

even has that slight anxiety
Sydney now provokes:
the praying group
in the seats near hers,

(yike!)—the train
"going too fast"

(tho she means
'too fast' for her

to *see* something she'd been looking for,
or at.)

Will they crash?

Granville . . . bombs . . . come to mind,
ready—as clues, if needed,
associations, a press of
meaning,

but the poem—her poem—
doesn't need them

#

Dis-ease.
I print the poem out
& go to the gym—half an hour earlier than
    usual—
a different bunch of faces.
One exercise I always hate
has me look at the carpet, as usual,
'noting'
that the machine moves forward
with each repetition
an eighth of an inch.

I always think
"continental drift",

"glacial".
(How fast

did they move?) I do it
last thing today.

Old Jack had the weights I use.
I went away.
Came back.

The lightest thing I lift—

but for him I think
the heaviest. He is

frail—early 90s.
Catching the lift

up & out
afterwards,

a young woman from
Hyatt administration

makes conversation with me.
She's in tightly corsetted clothing

heels, black stockings—the make-up, the
    hair etc—"professional"
(not dumb professionally,
but "a functionary" &
"impersonal"). Plump.
A look that always reminds me
of Gaston Lachaise sculptures.
((Which I never liked—a name I haven't
        thought of for decades.))
But she's okay.
(Who wants to stand
there in silence?)

How long have I been coming, etc?
"How long has the Hyatt
been here?" I ask,

an unintendedly
rhetorical rejoinder.

17 years, she thinks.
                    In
17 years I could
drive that machine
right across its corner of the gym.
An achievement of sorts.
                    Next
I leave the gym,
pick up the mail,

buy breakfast yoghurt,
order coffee.
I check Pam's poem again.
In the mail
a letter from her. That's
surely her handwriting.

Which turns out to be
publicity

for a reading she'll give—
sent, I think, in
the expectation

I'll like the image used—
that I hold now, in my hands—
& I do like it.
    I remember
other train poems, each one
clears its throat softly,
stands patiently,

reminding me
of its presence: Slessor's—
'Night Ride', &
'South Country'—

Auden, Larkin

(Auden's vivid, yet too true, too
typical, realism—

a mixture of Poussin's classicism
& the English, village cosiness—

Larkin's determinedly
'down' iteration, of

'the small-change of life',
of 50s Britain,

for one who means
to be disappointed).

Pam's poem is now.
And me? Am I now, too?
I am now

'going to work'
in a minute, finishing a

coffee up—or letting it
cool—reading stuff in

various papers.
Across the road,

in the silence imposed
by the glass & closed doors
of *Tempo* cafe,
bulldozers knock the cinema down,
& pile it
into one corner,

people go past
not exactly like

(but not un-like, either)
the women in Kirchner's Berlin streetscapes,
modern, busy, stylish
(style-*less*

in some cases).
The intro to a book I just finished
tells me that the author used edit—
"for the Princess Caetani"—a phrase I love—
"the *Botteghe Oscure Review*"—
a name I always loved,
(& used to joke about:
I liked the idea of a magazine
called *Boutique Oscuré Grotesque*)—
surprised when I got to Rome
to find it was the name of a street
—a street of 'shops'—that were all,

of course,
in shadow
(oscure).
Am I of now, or does this

all tie me
to a dead past—

like the cinema they're knocking down—
Garden of the Finzi-Contini—

the book in question—
like that?—
like Kirchner?

Berrigan & Pam
keeping me,

just, (maybe),
in the present.
"You're on, Mr Bolton,"
I imagine a voice saying
after a loud

but conventionally polite
knock.

       In this dream
I sit before a mirror,
I guess,

ready to go on.
A comedian? a singer?

My favourite version of the scene
was in *The Jolson Story*,
a movie I saw repeatedly,
as a kid: my dad loved it.

Screened with
tedious regularity.

The main act
is of course drunk
& out of it.

So young 'Al', the understudy,
goes on:
& a brilliant career begins.
The movie offers the cliche
straight.
Life. . . . Reality ('?')

—*a la* Poussin, Auden,
. . . a la *Hollywood?*
I grab the post office mail,
grab my stuff,
make off to work—
the aesthetic coal-face

of the Experimental Art Foundation—
new, relevant, current (!) —
me, that is. Well, the Experimental
                    Art Foundation, too.
Pam's poem in my hand—
& the card—with the image she sent—
backward-looking, modern.

THE DEATH OF BIG VOICE ODOM

for Peter Bakowski

Voice Odom
drove thru late
rush hour traffic.

At the first lights
that allowed him
time removed his

coat, placed it on
the seat beside,
flexed his

shoulders, against the
braces he wore, peered
into the rain & dark,

past the wipers
shunting back & forth—
figured it would snow—

searched idly
on the dash
for a bill he thought he saw,

near a photo of
wife & kids, taken
at his sister's. Unpaid,

the bill tugged at
some part of his brain.
Instead, earrings,

flyers, paperclips,
tickets,
a cassette or two,

an old 'police
procedural'—title
Heartstopper—sunglasses, an

ad that had him
appearing again
with Jimmy Dawkins—

incorrectly as it
turned out: the gig
fell thru—things

that reminded him
of who he was,
the public self

he was on his way to be,
across town,
thru traffic.

He pulled into the parking lot,
outside the club, a sudden
tightening in his chest,

parked, rested his
head against the wheel.

WHAT GOES ON?

I wonder how Crab is.
I wonder how Tub?
                    Maz —
what is *she* doing —
                    & Michael?
Cath
        would be long
in bed by now —
for her early-morning
start tomorrow. She
rang this week. We
both write.
                    It is 1 a.m.
Crab is probably going on, about now,
at the *Cargo Club* — or is drinking,
or watching television somewhere. If the latter
then Mary might be with him, or will be
early to bed and next morning
        appear:
in the kitchen washing her hair —
after an early morning swim, coffee
at the *Flash*, some expedition with Mill.
Millie will be bonging on   or drinking   or
dancing somewhere. Seb plays football
and should be in bed — though you never know.
I guess I am doing what I always do —
in their minds — I am in a room somewhere
(John's), writing, playing music — the *Velvet Underground* —
drinking drinks (retsina) thinking
of them.

POEM (WHAT'S BEST)

Actually, a
week into work—after
the holidays

              (the
weekend
     . . . &
Monday off)—
& finally
I am relaxed
happy even
            at what?
tho that is what's best
about it
          —that funny
flower
       that
grows outside my window
for one

associated now
with a particular friend,

Cath beside me, reading,
writing,
        kids at home, in
the back room
watching a movie
       (Anna
            Gabe)

         — their
disputes so loud &
quickly resolved—
         (Hayley,)
(Alex
      —the neighbouring kid—still a child
while the others are grown.
)

        The flower
is a yellow, creamy
white
    a bell
inside which is
a jam-red
stamen

     enough
to point up
the translucent
white surround.

    The bush has
sometimes two or
three flowers—
usually one, or none—
and not always open.

Cool weather, after a week in the 40s
the breeze moving through the room

via the windows
                        opened out
—into the yard,
the street—

The street-light—
                        moonlike,
(except that it is
always there—& like
a book design, that
you hardly notice)

(a streetlight
                on the cover of a
book by Celine, in fact.
                        That I had once.
          Do I have it
still?)
          I think 'moon-'
(rather than 'street-light')—

until we
go to sleep,

and then it
peers in
—*too bright*—

so unvarying it is
not the moon.

Though I go to sleep. No
mozzies tonight. My little
new fan—secondhand—a
Hecla (*"By Hecla it's good!"*
their slogan in the 60s). It
runs — silent.
                        The lines,
of Cath's

—pages of type,
held up in front of her—

they parallel the broader
black & white
of the top she wears

(—bought in Italy,
knitted).
                        My feet
are bare, uncovered,

on the bed, the
bottom sheet a
pale *crème de menthe,*

the top one *a 'scrawl' of
white cotton*—from
the days of heat before—
how it looks now.

Cath puts out her light—
just me now & the benevolent
streetlight coming thru the bamboo,
darker cloud
massing near the moon,
the wind coming up
to rustle the bamboo
tinkle the distant wind chime in the kitchen

then I go—open or close
windows, drink a glass
of water—
look,
from the bed, for the streetlight,
the moon—will
one have supplanted
the other?

POEM (WORRY, WINSOME)

*"Yuri's arrived. They seem to be
holding him in customs."* — *Gabe at Heathrow*

Cath's in bed
beside me writing
poems
2
that answer
Janet Charman's.
I sit arms
folded looking
sightlessly
& thinking.
"Sightlessly" seems
not the right word:
I *am* thinking.
But the things I see
imprint themselves
well enough—
so that
I will remember them
later.
(The particular pattern
on the bed cover:
sprigs of
olive leaves raised
so they catch the light
the birds in the
bird poster on
the door, the dark
of the window. It is
11 PM. The

light across the
street.) What
is Kurt doing, I think.
It might be hard
to make art
unsupported,
no one to talk to, his sons
young teenagers.
I guess he sees them
most weeks. Of course
he might be at a party
laughing, telling a joke.
(I think of him isolated.)
In a poem I wrote once
I imagined
phoning him—
late at night: would
he pick it up
or would it wake
Sarah, his partner?
Would he be in his studio?
Now I worry is
he there too often,
or that he is
too unhappy
to paint. I am reading
Delacroix—
the journals—slowly—
because of Kurt,
who was reading them

when I last saw him.
Greg & Jen,
Michael, Pam—(Laurie!)—
what are they up to?
or Sal? Steep
the soul
in beautiful things,
Delacroix says, &
noble deeds
& work calmly.
I steep myself
in the art of
Ron Padgett,
or did—when
I last felt like this.
(*There* is the joke—
"Ron Padgett",
"beautiful", &
"noble things". But really
I do think he is,
& on reading him
I sometimes write something
impersonal & clear & funny.)
Anna has just texted
& Cath reads it to me.
I know I
won't ring anyone
—too shy—
too unwilling
to leave my head space.

Texting
I should get into.
I hope they're all well.
Sal, Laurie,
Pam, Kurt,
Michael & Di,
Greg & Jen, their
kids. Our
kids! Cath keeps
a record
of funny texts from them
copied from her
phone memory:
Anna in Tasmania, the
boys in England,
Gabe waiting at Heathrow
for his brother Yuri.
"How many cavities
can one man have?"
he asks at
the delay,
time slipping by.

III ✳

POEM ("And Now here I am")

And now
here I am

lines & lines
after this poem should've begun

A curiously pleasant
but thwarted day, I

realize,
after I
have thought: "But what
have I 'done'

       (Apart
from work, which I am
paid to get done?)
I have

come home,
slept
played a tape
of Joanne's,

Thought :
about taping
—with her,
& Craig,
       played
Miles Davis

          —for the first
time Seriously
in a couple of years
          —by

seriously I mean
"it worked"

I am
Under its spell.

          More sleep.
& I awoke — to find

Sally & Mary
watching TV a

bit of quiche left
they tell me

in the kitchen
which I

go
to eat.

TV
is terrible
so I get my new bike out
my old, newly fixed

bike
& ride it

9.
30 at night

the just past full
moon no-

where yet visible, the
sky alight, the city

humming the
air

just mildly cool
to ride in

        And return:
to Micky & a joint, which
she quite calmly
produces—along

with a little commentary—
which we smoke

while Sally
fixes her shoes &

we go on talking.
On

TV Richard Chamberlain
craps on, soberly,

—*"Shogun"*—
& we talk over it
occasionally stunned
By the music

which every
so often "swells"—

distinguishing
the *'pregnant'* silences—

then are Blasted, into
a frenzy of

Silence
&

Agitation
When Sally switches

To film of natives—
piercing holes
in babies' faces, for Decoration.

        Micky
is about to leave & this

seems so entirely Reasonable :
when they become more peaceful :
& we all
calm down again.

Then the
natives get stoned!

which is
also pretty violent:

(bit of vomiting)
but we are 'with' them

& see
this one

thru—to the end
                    skip
Channel 2's
good-night

speech, & tune in
to REAL crap . . .

When Michele comes in!
—to borrow

money
For her taxi—home

From work, where there has been
'a Disaster',

which she is quite calm
about—but we

talk it thru.
It isn't

Her Fault, which is
True. But 'the

Place where she works'
'Are Idiots'

&
"who *knows*"
what THEY think?

And here I've finished
the bottom

of my second page
& realise—

both pages curl
across to the right, looking
pleasant,

but weird, like some crazy
Japanese—
a sort of abbreviated 'J',

of writing,
down each
page

And now I draw it
I realise "I really

am stoned"—it goes the
opposite way, to a J, and I thought,

briefly,
& intensely
before, about
what letter

curved that way

Now it is later
And I am writing this.

NOTES

Duty Chart—Part One & Part Two — I had had to write about friends, covering the period 1979 to 1982, for an exhibition—*Coalcliff Days*—that focused on our activities at that time. 'Pola' though, is a dog: she features in a number of these poems.

Two Melbourne Poems — begins with a sense of dislocation, that felt odd & inexplicable but worth trying to put a finger on, the usual feeling that can accompany giving a reading in a different town—probably to do with how busy I had been over that time—& how long it had been since I had visited Melbourne. Friends put me up for the last few days at their place out of the city, at Kangaroo Ground. There was a final reading and, on the way, a visit to Heide Gallery to see work by Ken Whisson, Danilla Vassilieff, and photos of the Heide set in their youth.

2.12.08 for Philip Whalen—"Here it comes again, imagination of myself"—the line is Philip Whalen's.

And Willing, Willing — the Meaghan in the poem is Meaghan Morris, with her word, "mixity".

Faces At Night — Bored with the distraction of my own reflection, I imagine the faces of my friends as *they* write (John Forbes, Pam Brown, Cath Kenneally, & others)—friends, but also the faces of some I have never seen.

A Friend Of His Dad's—Walter Bakowski, son of Peter & Helen.

In John's Room—a stay with John Jenkins in Brunswick, Melbourne. I must have been reading a book on Guston while at John's, and listening to a Velvet Undergound tape, that ends, for contrast, with Nancy Wilson's 'This Bitter Earth'.

It's Come To This — formerly titled 'A Silly Bugger', written in the late 90s in a Turkish restaurant in Melbourne's Sydney Road, Brunswick, over a plate of okra. The Larry Fagin book was *Rhymes Of A Jerk,* published 1974.

In Two Parts (Enlisting With The Moderns) — feeling ebullient (had I just read Berrigan's poem again?) I took up the cudgels for John Forbes—&, of course, myself—against the real & imagined enemies of the new.

Things To Do On The Island — on Bruny Island, clearly. It was an American poet I usually like whose new book I found disappointing, not Greg O'Brien's. His was terrific—though it took me ages to do the drawings.

"Hi, Small Bug!" — Issa, Japanese poet, 1763–1828. Alex & Penny: old friends I had not seen for very many years.

Late At Night—Bruny Island — I feel John Forbes would have liked O'Keefe's commentary. But John died too early to hear it—while, not following cricket, I missed it almost entirely.

New Way of Worrying — maybe I am conflating two generations of Trintignants into one career?

Re *Peter Black* — poet Greg O'Brien suggested I write something on Black for the New Zealand magazine, *Sport.*

Salute ("I wonder what Seb") — Seb Dickins, whom I've known since he was . . . ten? & I was thirty-two and had moved into a share-house he was part of, along with younger sister Millie, mother Mary Christie, Michael Zerman, Sally Forth, Emma & Wil Balfour, Michele Johnson, Mick Clark, Michael Snelling, & others. Seb now lives in Bondi.

Sanctuary — for my wonderful friend Julie Lawton.

Starting near the Cakeshop — a study of prejudices, assumptions & distances between people, on a day when I was not well enough to engage.

Transport / Train Ride — The poem mentions an image Pam had sent. I have forgotten now what it was, what it looked like. The author of *Garden of the Finzi-Contini* was Giorgio Bassani—it was he who edited 'for' the Princess Caetani.

Voice Odom, The Death Of — This is fiction, totally imagined, tho Odom—whose singing (on the Jimmy Dawkins release *All For Business*) I like a lot—did die, of a heart attack?

What Goes On? — written (in the late 80s) from John Jenkins' room in inner city Melbourne, imagining what my Adelaide crew are up to.

What's Best — from 1996 or so?

Poem (Worry, winsome) — Cath (Kenneally)'s book *Eaten Cold* 'answers' by various means the poems in New Zealand poet Janet Charman's volume *Cold Snack*.

Poem ("And now / here I am / lines & lines after this") — much as I liked this poem I suppressed it: it would seem so entirely a 'stoner's' poem, or maybe I doubted its value. But I like it still. From the early or middle 80s.

www.ingramcontent.com/pod-product-compliance
Lightning Source LLC
Chambersburg PA
CBHW030939090426
42737CB00007B/484